THE WAYS OF THE MONSTER

JAY BESEMER

the operating system print//document

THE WAYS OF THE MONSTER

ISBN: 978-1-946031-42-6
Library of Congress Control Number: 2018948571
copyright © 2018 by Jay Besemer
edited and designed by ELÆ [Lynne DeSilva-Johnson]
layout assistant: Lori Anderson Moseman

is released under a Creative Commons CC-BY-NC-ND (Attribution, Non Commercial, No Derivatives) License:
its reproduction is encouraged for those who otherwise could not afford its purchase
in the case of academic, personal, and other creative usage from which no profit will accrue.

Complete rules and restrictions are available at: http://creativecommons.org/licenses/by-nc-nd/3.0/

For additional questions regarding reproduction, quotation, or to request a pdf for review
contact operator@theoperatingsystem.org

This text was set in Avenir, Minion, Franchise, and OCR-A Standard.

The cover image is a detail from "Alfred Hitchcock Presents," by Rupert Glimm (acrylic mixed media on wood panel). Used with permission of the artist. More at www.rupert-glimm.blogspot.com

Books from The Operating System are distributed to the trade by SPD/Small Press Distribution, with ePub and POD via Ingram, with production by Spencer Printing, in Honesdale, PA, in the USA.

> Your donation makes our publications, platform and programs possible! We <3 You.
> http://www.theoperatingsystem.org/subscribe-join/

the operating system
www.theoperatingsystem.org

THE WAYS OF THE MONSTER

2018-19 OS System Operators
CREATIVE DIRECTOR/FOUNDER/MANAGING EDITOR: ELÆ [Lynne DeSilva-Johnson]
DEPUTY EDITOR: Peter Milne Greiner
CONTRIBUTING EDITORS: Kenning JP Garcia, Adrian Silbernagel, Amanda Glassman
UNSILENCED TEXTS ASSISTANT EDITOR/TRANSLATOR: Ashkan Eslami Fard
SERIES COORDINATOR, DIGITAL CHAPBOOKS: Robert Balun
JOURNEYHUMAN / SYSTEMS APPRENTICE: Anna Winham
ASSISTANT EDITOR/ACCESSIBILITY MANAGER: Sarah Dougherty
SOCIAL SYSTEMS / HEALING TECH: Curtis Emery
VOLUNTEERS and/or ADVISORS: Adra Raine, Lori Anderson Moseman, Alexis Quinlan, Erick Sáenz, Clarinda Mac Low, Bill Considine, Careen Shannon, Joanna C. Valente, Michael Flatt, L. Ann Wheeler, Jacq Greyja, D. Allen, Charlie Stern, Joe Cosmo Cogen, Bahaar Ahsan, you

The operating system is a member of the **Radical Open Access Collective**, a community of scholar-led, not-for-profit presses, journals and other open access projects. Now consisting of 40 members, we promote a progressive vision for open publishing in the humanities and social sciences.

Learn more at: http://radicaloa.disruptivemedia.org.uk/about/

contents

[part one] 7

[part two] 55

[part three] 93

[part one]

How to understand heavy little word *I*?

What is being said & from what mouth?

Some of a body's things taken to extreme as though a vision had only one source-eye.

I-word small as a maggot takes hold, packs the light into a deft animal sincere as wrong.

Speak & be known but as what & by what? Make this like why, & shed it.

That isn't the right opus. To say [ ], and mean it.

Non-freeze pattern in sound registered as pixels on a [ ].

Today I practice holding my breath. Knowing some embroidered apron, handwork press.

Today I practice a vast hunger. Territorial eye, registered as pixels on a dying Jumbotron.

Juicy little nicety, don't you step on hope.

I'm a man of the people, but which people?

When in degrees of adjustment & focus the shortness of breath distracts our frail reasoning.

That pretty leaning toward the pastries. That dialogue between wet & dry.

Contact points corroded with sugar & aspic, exuding neurotransmitters.

Mistakes get made. Families increase exponentially. Algae blooms choke out any other possibilities.

Life swirls in confusion, bastes itself in its own juices.

We dip our hands into troughs of blood, smear our faces with it.

Coat our thighs with orange peel. Irrational behavior.

There's the sound. It's a mud pie to the side of the head.

In fairness, if not in practice, the gap between listening & looking, so we're told.

If I smoke this in your face that means you owe me.

Have to wonder what that looks like, how meaning gets assigned there, & the deliberate

    choice to turn away from delusion.

Pitting fragments & adjustments against singularities of certitude.

How I haven't been swimming in decades but somehow never left the water.

What is mourned is not the cage but what was allowed to slip between its bars.

What is not permitted a man who wants to be perceived as one among many, as many within one.

Sometimes all that is left is to take comfort in the part of speech that grows.

I see my cruelty, the ruthless blankness of rage.

What is mourned is not the cage but the tenderness I must keep from beloved friends, like the horrible violence of my fear.

Every day I awake instantly catapulted into the place of living where adjustment is

    inescapable & unending.

I awake at the wall where something always starts, always sets its sights on something else

    just over my shoulder.

I awake itching & dimly remembering a plan or a name.

There is a name that once was given to me. Maybe that's the one.

The average of all the things that once quantified me for others, now converted to obsolete

    un-provable theorem.

Long apologies pulled from the face as a protective measure.

Today's moan ringing in our ears, tonight's moon working early.

Nothing is easy. The words are absent. The gold still asleep in the safe.

Betweening on paper made criminal so we each make our differences & crack your files & safes.

Make you a promise without a schedule.

Make payment as demanded from one pocket to the other.

Some tyranny happens slowly, a face at the window or a pat on the back.

Description can't be prediction, a maze of conditions we wander as ants wander their

      homes & habits.

We also live inside earths of our making & adapting.

If love vacates the environs what is left in the picture? Look for the subject in the pattern.

Or look at absence, begin to differ.

All stop. Hesitation on the edge of action.

Here's the same old rift between the thing desired & the movement toward it. Still so terrified of the want. Still so intimidated by hope.

Strange failure, disappointed cart placed well before the horse that might take us out of it, as though disappointment itself were the goal.

No mere mess to clean up but a whole abattoir of pleasures butchered.

There must be something else.

Love my aggression & my little star-flavored openings.

Talk to me. Everything we know is altered in the process.

Love my aggression. Spy on me, I beg you.

Evaluate my rightness as a candidate, a new recruit, a target demographic.

What you understand is not what I am. What you fail to understand.

The hoop of prefrontal work, the wing that doesn't close.

But in a way that could mean freedom.

Shut away with the wolf cub & the pale drum of blistering desert, the bin of beads.

There are many ways to walk from here to here. There are many maps.

Take a harness from the hook & rub it against your cheek. The ring of keys. My open fly.

Through the window the sky's voice comes. The emergency sound, a basket of rattlesnakes.

We are only two little lights. What is our way now?

The wake of the action spreads in the past as well as the future.

That's incorrect, people say. A woo-woo kind of thing, dismissed like a subaltern in

    disgrace.

Punishment takes many forms. I don't have enough wrists for all the world to slap.

Once I was a child. Yes, I admit to that. White hair & staring eyes too blue for my face,

    a procession from one fall to the next.

Once I was a child but I am no longer.

The time for dismissal has passed or has not yet come.

In a word's space a fire of movement is contained & everything else is potential.

You need this. The things you watch for, my chaotic movements, the vocal idiocy of

    misapprehension.

Stumble through a barrage of names & honorifics & facial expressions.

Yes, I'm only doing this to make you uncomfortable but you can turn that into a selfie if you

    want.

See, next to me you are obviously solid in your position. No questions asked. Bigger

    sureness than doubt.

Let's move on.

Covered in potatoes, eloquence, differentiation in a pocket like a dream book.

The terrible phrases that make you.

Car, bank, aspiration of. Irritation ways.

This mark on the hand, this dear thing.

Licenses & abilities noted. Cargo sorted & applied to tariff.

Run from noise like a dog & arrive thereby in some other lineage.

Arrested, crowned with vines, placating as a nursery.

Peril, many kinds.

Orbit skull like moths orbit lamp, replete as a barrel of eels.

Many kinds, some are not from within. Peril a parlor of predators demanding all say yes,

        pasting labels to briskets palm oil a spiny spiny deer skull.

The emphasis on tremble, the odor of pillbug.

Take big turkey wing in hand, lick the feathers down in a postal way.

Peril from the soles of the feet on up.

Now what are the names of those bones? Tell me.

No waterboard, no tea with Uncle Values.

I'll thank you to keep off the nipples & the questing.

The sociopathic dugout never more full than a hall of mirrors.

Time in the stomach grows loud, a beard of stones & walnuts slaps the chest like a

    classroom.

Makes bonny bonny sound travel, coursing the hares, klepto-crypto-governmental nodes.

Wearable data device improves productivity so where were you my fine fellow & where

    was your umbilical rot, the passive voice you haul from garage to garage?

If I exist unchecked how can you ever reproduce? How can you maintain the card games &

aqueducts & exchange of capital?

If I exist unchecked how can you insist that your offspring do your bidding?

How can a person ever again be the equal sign between means & ends?

How can you keep pretending that the digital thumb has meaning? That your currency has

value?

That I, your monster, am really unlike you?

If I exist unchecked, why must that hurt you? Recognition is painful but not harmful.

Honor yourself, for I do you no dishonor.

Solve problems of inclusion by putting myself in the picture, a soft landing resulting from a soft opening. Jargon makes mud pies.

Freeze outside the gates as the shutters click. What energy all this takes.

My reservations under the old name, body banked up like a fire around the new.

Look at the names I used to know & wonder if the door really is closing & if it is, why.

Is it because of who I am or who I'm about to? Or some sort of supposed-to-be I never was quite?

I'm not lost or confused. I may well be a traitor but I do live here & love this place just like you.

Waking up.

Displacement steeped green with luminous sorrow.

Today the day of exile when silence is forbidden. A ghostly horse & carriage escapes from a tin, haunting & cold.

Find the way. Find the silence denied.

Two palms pressed to the earth. Blue eyes turned to fierce gems.

Lives not extinguished but lost to fear & shame, to incomprehensible obedience.

One cry left at the bottom of the throat & it is somehow enough.

The doll of blemishes sits to wait eager for blame, a tasty exorcism pushed into it.

The fright of the populace, questions that amount to unmaking pounded into semi-person like studs into a pole.

Crust of hatred collects on a face, a shell of tainted sugar.

A wall of dull eyes watches, bored by suffering.

Indifferent flesh carried around an empty breath, unacquainted with thought.

Blurt & burn, in between as decision gets made.

How this happens. Temper chaos with a little bed, a little noise caught in the cheek.

A little dollar boy driven by fuck by battery acid running away from the news that he is a

    lump of salt in a seed bank.

No shout can be loud enough in this din.

The voice scabs over & sinks below ground & that's fine with him.

Disintegrate these people make them helpless be the lord of everything.

Without a single vertebra to call your own, power false in the mind, disguising your own

    absolute inadequacy.

Count on us to paint you sunny & good. Wrong.

Adult males, solitary, attendant to territory.

Beings & others.

The will of the water or else the din of change.

When we listen we hear what? Mice. False bats trembling in the trees as the wind comes up.

Spotted knife of the gaping trap. Some thick leg in gabardine.

You have your eye on that implacable enemy, seven-ringed event & surroundings to map.

The shapes you've been trained to watch out for.

Don't wish, don't sit in a corner out of reach of the sky.

When you breathe listen for the horses in your chest.

When you breathe the blood reaches out to the air that holds you.

Everything in the body matters. The light that licks the skin of your cheek. The soft need of
    your hands at work in your center.

You have your eye on some mighty aura. How hopeful it is to be wrong!

The way you mate, & are boring.

The compulsive affection function.

The way you purpose. Purpose me arms & bag of knives.

The yaw of cinder tossed over a balcony, turkey fat rubbing rubbing in palms & sea dollar.

Straight people obsessed with straight women binding their breasts for art. Passing as men

      for money etc., returning to factory presets once they get what they want.

Purpose me. Million uses for thing/dude.

The trope of this exposed bastard. Alligator in bed, albino & stretching.

Sanity in a jaw & backlighting.

The fuck of it. Stretch of road drawn onto flesh. Acne, hair.

Why would I identify as your goddamn creamy goodness?

Like some sausage exposé, two-tiered, noise & smell.

You've got a horse, you've got a different color. You've got a sideline in artisanal planet-
      killers.

What could you want with me? Am I made of diamonds or angus beef? Am I Portland-
      based & sustainable?

Is this a hidden-camera show? You want I should navigate my flap-fronts at you, little
      darling? My tyrant dance?

Something like love, something like love wiped off your menu.

Tomorrow, deep cage, deep brimming causal sequence.

Dread creates weariness. I have taken my muscles in hand & given notice.

The bards sit empathically alert & patient in preparedness.

I want to move slowly & with great forethought.

I drain my sources, my withering glare.

If I am a sentence what then, what then? If I am a man, what then?

If I am a fabrication, whose hand?

The dial of definition drained of all power.

When in the eye of the beholder I have no idea what to do.

These questions asked, always a variation on a theme.

A confrontation with that family of hidden expectations.

A vast boa of yearning curves behind the sacrum, pushes me here & there with arms spread

    wide, to gasp in pain for the sacrifice of older intimacies.

The price of inclusion is to erupt in sticks & stones & chitin.

So few permissible to touch, so few mouths to take my word.

Chokehold. Wait for this to become that.

Time & obedience & the fist of authority beneath your jaw.

Some endowed person licensed to tell you what you are & to make you be that to justify

    their actions upon you.

These murdered men & I, the poster formerly known as freedom.

You must be kidding me, to assume it has no effect on my body.

No shout can ever be made clear enough.

No posture ever submissive enough. There is no end to it.

Strung: a bow maybe or a lute or what if a reference to a past position or state of strength?

Descriptors possessing tenses, tensions & why not? Everything else does these days.

Every window about to die outward raining itself onto the street because it just can't

    anymore, it just can't.

Don't you know how that feels? That sense of failure in plain view, everyone knows it & you

    just can't admit it.

Strung like a runner bean onto its support.

Move along from one obligation to the next. Rust will consume us all in no time.

What is it, that sly little way of looking? The glance that bleeds.

Who is encumbered here, the one looking or the one almost-seen?

There is a question implied in that strange moment, a tongue licking doubtful lips.

Fear & desire are the same thing & no language holds that pledge the eyes make.

Pain, annoyance in suggestive tones.

Try to find the snap of the Taser in all this.

Try to find the departmental policy paper. Institutionalization of the means of harm.

The bag behind which the imperative is hidden.

A populace with hands lifted. A populace kneeling in the street. A populace stripped & ordered to die.

A destroyed man erased from humanity, less protected than a child's chalk drawing on the sidewalk.

Stamp of approval, cosigning the apocryphal cherry tree of bisected pain.

These stories beloved of landfill battery boxes lusting for corroboration.

Time was, any little piece of shit could recite the jingo jingo way & feel it right here, here in the heroic breast. Meant to be the diff between man & less-than, not American.

Some here still sit in that tent & muster, rocking forward & back with their thumbs on their apples.

Is it any wonder everybody's eyes get smaller & smaller while worms bite, mechanized licking taking hair off the top, in the interim?

Automated aerial matchstick errors from here to eternity like a vampiric idea come home at last to stay.

I don't like your media, your hypertrophy.

The pangolin that beats in my ribcage says you've crossed the line.

Get in a circle & duck duck goose.

This mulligatawny of mine drowns out the pumpkin fucking spice of latter-day demographic crosswinds.

The point is, I'm history.

All right, I'm made of money, which is why I never make any. This entity does not reproduce. You should know this by now.

Look at me will you? See my rhizome down around my ankles.

Accept this theory tendered like a slip of flesh, an engine.

Placed against the skull at the occipital overhang, humming.

In it now, like a sludge field.

A species of love for walking, walking, walking.

Travel in words alongside another who travels in words.

The silence one presses beneath one's coat like contraband. Clandestine space of poetry,

        surveillance. Printable guns to shoot plenty.

No danger from us, we are only marginalia. Mutually assured irrelevancies.

This love walking, walking in a city built with table salt, our backs striped by rosebud whips.

Love walking toward you, hands out, palms forward.

These you lean into, a wind of a moment or a choice like the lost gloves of last year's leaves

    on a dormant tree.

These that are not poison but choices not yet tried & the empty sun of the past.

The trial without resolution totaling its thick testimony, its dust & nails.

Always one last fruit in the bowl, to force the hand around.

Sheaf of muskets driven into the ground. A bomb filled with starlight.

Saw this & thought of you.

The question of anger & its uses, a packet made of heavy iron paper holding dust of

        happenstance ghost-animations.

Emanations of tiny rage.

Touch it into open. Listen. When will it be enough?

When will you look me in the eye & accept that I am who & what I say I am?

Everywhere I go I am that suspicious package posters tell you to watch for.

Want to tell me what it is I'm holding?

Illuminate the corners of the drought at least.

Can these forces collect or extinguish or sometimes know?

Thought of you because you always had so many questions. So hardily enveloping those

        bones of bell.

The season of deficiency now under way with the characteristic pallor of its front matter.

Soul-death rides in on a manic tin monkey walloping its cymbals together, making various

nogs.

We have recourse only to calendar choking.

We are new battles. A portent would probably pass us by.

In the event that our hearts break under the strain, you may see our tree walk into some

other sense.

A part of our betrayal paid for, no language left to justify us in your eyes & we know this.

You must let us go & will not & every day the shell hardens.

Horses stamp & steam on the hill & we burn more & more brightly.

Find a strange innocence in this.

These procedures of parley with unexpected animals, moving into a known & knowing

        body becoming older & younger simultaneously.

There is an ark of language not all of it human.

There is a world once insensible now present & tempting in its matter.

How to hear the others when they speak, the hiss & bellow of the lesson.

The flash of motion. The silence, transformation's only voice.

All the discs we don't buy are transformed into sequins & lamé jeggings.

This happens independently, without human effort.

Tremendous change, product turns inside out, philosophy for all to see.

But there is a way it could also go, a mathematical locomotive, a palm tree waiting to

    become the shade it promises.

Potential in matter. Bodies stretch from one state to another, all unfixed & tending toward

    the edges of the universe & we too & all we make.

A sparkle in the eye. Fruit.

Deepest sky.

We wish to part company with the vast unlovely gasworks of received expectations. Those claims of duty without substance.

The structures shimmering in mirage. Unclear manifestations half-notion, half-rust.

Florescence of calcination or weeping condensate liars.

Embedded bacterial colonies.

Has nothing worked for you? Have you tried it all only to stand with your nose in the crotch of two scaly walls, stymied by punctuation & gravy?

Join us, rip your shirt, bare your desperate nipples. Have a heart.

Stop making pudding from self-defeat & move your own earth for a change.

There was something about flowers.

There was also the need to tell stories about a man others knew.

There was a door passed again & again. Air moist with mantra.

Feet on pavement working points into lines.

There is a way of seeing & living that opens us up, soaks us in the universes & the earth that

       made us.

There is a way to recognize the love that penetrates us.

Begun from stone, now light. A man others knew, a body in flower.

Believe in me. I am the man with small hands usually open.

I am the son of the question & the wheel.

I am the paint on the freezing lamp, mantle always covered in soot. Trust my teeth & my

    apples. In dreams you have held them.

Raw flesh & raw wind burying the written word.

Each knife that speaks grows duller with every breath.

Fruit of language held in small hands. Tough & veined. Usually open.

This taste of ink forever on my tongue.

I am the man with a heart of grain.

With blood-borne fire.

Believe in me. I can do nothing but love.

When you ask about the soul-point all the matter rushes into it.

A dust of ignorance coats the tongue we share. Darkness reconsiders us, what we are doing.

Who could roll in that question now, the light shrieking in the tree, so bitter?

No essence here, no coat to hang on it.

How hard things form, condensed around the wick of maybe, or crust & scab a scum over

    slow fluid, weary in its claim to being.

A banner year, a sprig of parsley.

Fingers in the ears to trouble trouble.

Who cares when mud is made?

A desk pushed into the corner for the happenstance to stand on.

Make a shiny circle on the wall, make a bin full of napkins floss ostrich burgers. Remember
        ostrich burgers?

Too organized for my own good I look for a new canal.

Oh preternatural bronze crucible vibrating with hot, hot down the ages & eyes that spill
        cream & questions on the magnetized arm!

Who can steer the loam & bite the blossoms of the vine but you my dear?

When the wars end & the smoke recedes like the meniscus in a half-full glass, when my

        hands itch to carry this lamp or a benign weight into another room, my mouth will

        open & a maze of sound will emerge.

My eyes, ablaze with trust & potency, will fill with tears.

My skin will write its salt & its coins all across the sky.

Do you see? The things we fight for do fight for us as well.

The hair that stands at the back of my neck, the throat that fits the word as the plum fits

        the stone.

Embrace life & its bone, the things I cannot wait to claim, the now of it, my everything.

[part two]

This is what I know: the shape of anything can be changed.

What began as earth turns to sky. What began as ox turns to army.

To speak of a thing is also to change it, to take it into your mouth, to fill yourself with a

    thing you have named.

You & it becoming permeable in your speaking.

This is how our worlds shape us.

How word and world meet inside us.

How we become, & make ourselves matter.

Make bodies to move into. A secret. I'm giving it away.

Bodies like they say of work. Are you receiving?

Pull open the guarding flesh & let me enter.

Make space between words & let me enter.

Dream of enough spoons, enough blankets. Let me enter there, too.

I am the kind of man who seeps & stains, wicks up from the edges.

Put it on paper. I will saturate you as I saturate my own body.

At these times the body becomes a forest that runs right up to the edge of a cliff.

The body becomes a wheelbarrow loaded with defunct electronics.

The body becomes a display of antique scissors.

At these times the signals become impossible to interpret clearly.

Wind & rain combine into one single packet of data.

The body takes in but it does not give back.

The body tries out different positions, costumes, meanings.

There is no standard shape. We love.

The signals play as animals play. We continue to love.

The body lights itself from within.

Enchanted house. Enchanted lamp. Garden of spirits.

Somewhere cast vaguely about for a language or an origin.

To begin the emergence from pupa to imago. A recasting of one human creature from maturity to metamorphic indeterminacy.

Now the strange pore opens. The twilight of the known body descends.

The throb of need & the deed of knowing. Lessons of the reconfigured center.

A match for this daily fuse.

Nothing left but to envelop this becoming in pictures & words.

A fraught edge knifing through the most intimate space.

The very skin of this, the mask wrinkling & flaking in the sun.

A word sent far away, bleeding or spinning in the air.

My things, all.

Do you underneath? Do you perhaps? Do you peach basket?

The paraphrase is aphasic, the drip of need that drives this carriage.

I will bite your tongue. I will carry your toad in my hat.

The very skin, mask, spot I missed when shaving.

Word sent out for coffee, yet to return.

The fine line between hypo & hyper.

We can talk about it again & again but the truth migrates. The skin migrates, & the blood.

Look at this magnified world, exaggerated ad absurdum.

Place yourself in its frame, pop in & out of greenscreen.

Suddenly the stakes are inescapably high. Your life-&-death crosses mine. Eruption. It hurts.

My spines & scales push through soft skin.

From hypo to hyper. Slips of the blood that now determines my days.

In the dark, defenseless, keening with longing for a language that might make space for

    my body.

Nothing of the sort that fits in my mouth.

Reading between the bars, not between the lines.

To wit, understand that even love cannot function as protective talisman. That teeth & scales have purpose & must be so.

Auroras come fast & heavy now, as mud, lace unraveling, dissention at dinner over starters.

We go to look at Poussin's weird Arcadia, notice I'm the guy who isn't in the picture. & my opens, my mouth it does, out. A puzzle box.

Read between the bars like a cage you know, not like a pub. & I coat myself in tears & blood but it does no good. The real is really real. The real is really real. Tick, tock & toe in the door.

The hardness of the action & what it requires of me.

Tears, blood & all, cashed in, some mortgage of self-preservation.

There is a story about a woman who birthed a stone. I am that stone.

There is a story about a man given a stone to eat in place of his son. I am that stone.

There is a story about a man who controls others by inhabiting them, changing them to suit his will.

I am not that man.

This is a different story, a body constantly retold.

Pages printed & folded.

I am not the one who changes others. I am not the one controlled by will.

It is a fable, this body. Any body, a fiction permeable & permanent in revision, retelling.

The tea is the blood is the mixed metaphor.

In your lap your identity rests, curled round your sex like a serpent round a tree.

You believe in it. You believe in the squat cup in your hand, in the red liquid it holds.

You believe in the doubt with which you regard your emanations.

You believe in the certainty in the face the mirror gives you.

Yet in the cup you taste a thing or two you can't abide.

Think of an internal combustion engine, the controlled death propelling everyone forward.

The growl & burn of the blast of total desperation.

Up & down, flash, & gone. Again, again.

Sip. Identity. Sex in hand, up & down.

Your entire body a mixed metaphor.

That sex elephant in the room is my self-haunting. Can't let go of it, can't let go.

In each struggle there is a new foe auto-asphyxiating & wrong wrong wrong.

I put myself out there, like an eye.

A bundle of nerves, *c'est moi*, bouncing over my own cheek.

My cultivars can't yield. My organs shift.

I'm not ready, & yet that's all I am or can ever be: ready.

I touch my mouth & my name leaps out, a bird erupting from cover.

I cup my chin in my small thick hand. You would do it too this way.

My fingers move between my lips. I part my teeth. Seek my tongue.

Pinch & pull it forth to follow the bird of my name.

My tongue, my language. Wet fruit of words. Half a plum stretching to a phrase.

Pull it out slowly until it hurts.

This is one poem, one way to give a form to a thought thing.

One gift of body, one strong gesture, one strange seed shared man to man.

These things I'm not on the other side of. Assimilation or passing: see index.

Loneliness, well of: see index.

The word *penis* is spoken by someone else, causes discomfort. The word *sperm*.

Whole interrogations in hybrid-genre heterosexual discuss clitoral breathing, semaphore.

Folks say body tells what way to go up mountain & what some fucking valley means.

Where do the companion animals live? Where the urban metaphors?

Where do the spirit guides take the traveler by hand?

There are no more attempts at understanding.

Dry dry wood in a cone props itself up with assumptions.

Makes it for the cookpot hanging above & calling itself society.

It hit below the belt. Vision shrank & dimmed.

Next day, terror. The dilation of risk.

Now, a wheel of sweat rolls from head to toe & we are stinking for silence.

For some different feeling or some bit of question. Fabric of becoming.

Drowning in the illusion of business-as-usual.

Drowning in the vast noise of lies.

What is the heart & can it be read?

What is the self behind the gritty masks?

It is forbidden here to trust our bodies, to know their words through static, to love them.

There is no dispute with my blood. Make its poison into food.

This brick or that, becoming meat, becoming artichoke.

The heart pulls & pushes, big diamond spinning in my bones, strange & hard.

Close my eyes. Wrench a wild cry from my throat.

The tomorrow of me still on another page, my fingers wet with data.

Pants down, pants down.

Pants down. Are you upset?

Look here at this tuft, the strange skin. These are (pants down) hairs of light.

Move your mommytron trade out of my harmattan.

I want you to look here at these elements of meat, the bite of horror in my hand.

Pants down pants down move out of the frame for a moment. There.

Your habits will not make me a bunny or a syrinx. Give it up now.

You see here, it's just like you heard, just like you were told, just what you were afraid of.

The folds are filled, concavity rippling with otherness. Take your either or & go home.

They've been asking real bucket questions.

Nickel-words wrapping around tongue right at the root.

Making a pie out of patience, some speech forced out of the body.

Making fevers on the flesh.

Answers like great stones pushed out through the sinuses.

They've been looking askance as one looks at a mirage or a ship appearing on a noon

    horizon, listening to cracked lips form pain.

The meal of acceptance now only a smear on a napkin.

Something immobilized in this man, a horn of fear pinning the body to itself, alone.

I bring you my dangerous equipment & inescapable conditions.

I knock on your door. Word, lineage, treatment of my drift. Sad salad of sequential

    re-mapping.

I have news for you: my knife is extensive. My imp is perverse. My baubles are not coveted.

    My film is fading.

Flamingoes make pretty pretty. I smear my walls with sweat. I knock again on your door.

Call me a micromanager. Call me a creepy fuck.

In my boots my toes collude & my ragin' heart splits into a knowing grin. I'm here for you,

    baby.

Hand in glove, the skin folded across the current underneath, flowing.

A thing that exemplifies hurt & the ways we know it.

The childish cry in the space between the ribcage & the street.

Another apostrophe to hook under the clavicle.

Clavicle, something-key. Make your line.

I like to listen for your hand. In the word spoken by air & mechanism I listen for shapes
      made by fingers.

Tip of tongue between upper & lower incisors.

Something-key.

A beautiful day all endorphin. Can you lip it big?

I'd like to fold you over that railing like a pride flag. I'd like to spin you silly on my axis.

I'd like to suck your knuckle, genius.

No joke, the screen is dark & I left my animal at home.

I miss little eyes in the night so watch out for that.

My diabetic attitude trumps my arthritic temper.

My overbearing shelves & selves.

Whatever else I've got, you know I have good shoes.

Come down here & besmirch them.

Love my various & difficult monster.

Make noises like a sky full of inclinations.

In a walk away from a denatured child under which I had hidden, in a folding fortune-

    telling paper mouth, the predictive skirt fails yet again & these bare feet perform

    admirably.

Lick lick lick little monster.

Work that monkfish into a stone ripple jutting over the sea, into a lantern showing order &

    its punctuation.

Great holy monster beating, bone laid bare in the teeth of the day.

Some moments make a man long for stop-motion sequences & fur.

Night thunders you to sleep.

A gray gift hand reaches out to stroke the flesh below the awning of the ribs, to grip the hip

    the mouth of the west, the helm of yes & of need.

Holy monster sucking the fallen stars scooped in handfuls, rubbed into raw skin.

Wait for my capacity to arrive, to respond to your urgent hush.

Close these eyes. Open new eyes a moment later.

The gulf between seconds is a gulf between worlds.

In an eternity of flux the only tool is a pencil, a pencil for placing an arbitrary slinking line

    between something & something else.

Underneath that line sits the inexpressible, the terrible net of feeling that makes a scarecrow

    of the bones & drives its fat claw into this body again & again like some president's

    bulletproof car.

The graphite trail that shelters me is a limit.

When will it decay into some blur of particles loosed from their bonds, enter me,

    demanding?

Do you dare take that treasure from its pit?

Like a little child you hang your feet over the edge & spit between them.

The long line of your fluid makes a bullet soft as a worm.

One day your scar will become a nail. Your body will become a lamp. The treasure will

    become a city.

Your long bullet just another mute toy, solidified, half-buried, a pin through its sternum.

An unfortunate depth of fear. So, it begins again.

We try to stroke our bodies for comfort, lick our flesh into line, but where do we stop?

So many stories that end with one man lost & alone amid ruins. Desolation.

Foolish, hands open like fans at the end of paper arms, woven straw heart between the

        teeth.

Nothing left to take, not even a bow.

Loud shank of brittle understanding shifts beneath a wet garment.

The salt mask makes itself again.

Drown the selves in history again, helplessly.

In a place of half-light & reflection count the hairs emerging.

Take solace in this. The nature of panic has changed, you see.

No more a cask of serpents' eggs hatching in the belly, slow squeeze at the temples.

It is the blood, instead. The heart forced through the bones & into the hands.

The lungs impossible, too vast to move.

Been expecting this hazard to erupt for some time now.

Trembling in front of the calendar, forcing the issue, forcing perspective.

Pressed into some service like a man snatched at port.

Does it follow from this that I'd stop fighting? To what do I pledge loyalty?

To what do I align my compass? The taste of your earth so dry & simple, the reach of some

    cold flag?

Stretch my arms wide. Decide my moves in secret sequence. Forget everything.

Look: the beleaguered walk of the slow winter cockroach. Sleep waddling into & out of the body.

Nightmares & books that stack in your days.

Surround bodily needs with the fortifications of the mind. It isn't enough.

There's no protection from need. There is no escape from this absolute force. The meat demands. The pain erupts.

Without a body these things were so easily dispensed with.

Now you're a man in a sequence of negotiations.

Ache of hands & rasp of voice confirm.

Set up the ogham of daily dance. The embrace of this whole bed of flowers & veins.

Fern of blood coloring your face with surprise.

Attempt to smile using both corners of the mouth.

Difficult & surprising.

Begin with the thought that the face composes itself according to intent.

The evidence in contradiction.

Practice in front of a mirror. The body wants to lead.

Capture the result with a camera.

Uncertain message, half a fearful rictus, half a clown's leer.

Who are all these people staring through this bastard window?

Open the glad flesh with both hands.

Make methods, a baying hound or a falcon.

Put yourself there, & there. Pour the dust onto the bed.

You are the green & gold sound of the sunrise.

Tongue and breath fill your mouth, alight with thick flame.

The dim eye flutters open, awake.

How, spread on a surface, the body turns to potential or object.

The short central vibration as a making.

Field of hair, skin warm & abdomen tense, then relaxed.

There is a wilderness to become, a need for broad sequence from this to that, here to there.

    & grass tall heaving in the wind, how the body becomes this.

Sun-warmed groin, erection, sudden laughter.

Curious hands. The seeking, like an act of speech.

To say something is open, something grasped.

A break that becomes a resonance.

There is a mask of understanding we put on.

A fear of hair, of separation, of power or joy without betrayal.

A fear of appearing as we are in any moment.

Touch & commit to the body, spin the nurse of shame to face the wall.

Be & give, full froth & tongue.

Curious hands. Song & groan.

Baste that hard fire into the seams of my trousers.

Your work will soon be finished.

Tall gems & winter coffee & the dial tone of old.

Milk spurting from dizzy slits.

To groan with the paper & sand of it all. To wait by the window for the excuse to come.

Oh dear friend, I am on my knees to you & the room shudders once, twice. We are still.

Touch this reptile heart in strange skin.

Touch the open mouth making contact between species.

It's what was called to you.

A movement inside to enter dialogue with a process, hard to make a world out of or even
        press into the existing fabric of things.

A learning curve that looks suspiciously like the horizon.

Grounded & belly-mudded, make it new, make.

Make this too & this body & stand in the middle of things.

Here it is, what you called, it's coming.

That bad red roach walks up & down all day. Made of want & need & shine.

A friend to the hand, a friend to the blood.

A friend to the visions that wait for making.

Lives in the dark & doesn't sleep.

Breathes through its skin & grows & grows.

Walks up & down. Jerks when it speaks.

It speaks all over.

Walk in & alongside that unseen lizard man. Inhabit his contours even as he shifts.

Plane to plane. Planet to planet. Strangers without center, or n actors in search of.

Your emotions, his emotions.

You tell yourselves the time. Tell yourselves night is coming.

Camera directions. Night. Medical data points on each other's skin.

The reality of adjustment means strange intercourse.

There, not-there. Flesh, not-flesh.

Man, leaning toward sangfroid in a mediated endothermic body.

Dispassionate until the light comes.

[part three]

Some wild question aimed like a portent in a specific stream of events.

This sense of walking into a dispute already in progress, noises & audience shifting.

The strange way that action unfolds, to be swept under the carpet.

To hide beneath a leaf like a lost key.

From the stage there is a collapse of energies.

A statement then a demand.

One step, two beyond the expected dance

      & a man's hand turns, turns in the light to a boat or a dish

      & the words emerging from his mouth stretch into bands of fabric dripping with

      painful broth.

Blankness becomes audible. The terrified earth groans with us.

In terrible waves it opens. A sky or a mouth of news & rating.

The contractions of a reverse parturition.

No chance to track the movement of splendors or glint.

See the wind scatter the branches.

North north-east. Buildings dance in place.

Passing by, see a late rose imprisoned in the grill of a bad truck.

The air is soaked in ochre.

Stoneware waiting to shatter.

A circle of men, their hands over their heads.

Walk crust of filth baked into the street.

Walk oil scab spread over the sidewalk like a terrible quilt.

Walk stares of people. Eyes of drivers.

Walk cracked headlight of swaybacked pickup truck.

Walk negative-number confidence factor.

Walk stopgap humiliation of the methadone clinic.

Walk tiny dog & enormous master.

Walk screaming child.

Walk sun-bleached desperation of violence & blood effervescing painfully.

Walk timetable of development.

Walk burning skin.

Walk brilliant willow standing up to its hem in duckweed.

Walk ground singing deliriously of last week's flood.

There is a pathway beyond the steel & ice of terror & loss.

The strange scales on the holy tree, the walking tree of error.

There is a song the air sings here in this place of ending & absence, a boot & box song in

        which thoughts are taken from place to place & animals observe the changes in the

        earth's rotation.

Night is coming. It is a glass bead on the tongue, tasting of emptiness.

Outside the door it is 79 degrees. It's 73 in Los Angeles & in Paris.

These things matter. Rain matters in Paris, thirsty stones & bearded graves.

Sun pops on the glass towers of a place I do not know. Laughing trees.

This city leaps & stretches & falls like a jet of water.

Outside the door the same sun grips me by the nape of my neck, makes me desperate with

    lust.

I want the dirt & the flood.

I want the sharp voice of someone's little dog.

I want the musky blood of hope smeared across my chest & that long hand.

The Thames unrolls licorice-like, pangolin-sexy stretch.

There's a city somewhere in all this, maybe just meters away from us.

So well-played, tight dialogue plausibly rendered. Action is hard, in character.

What city is this? Can you be London if you've got a bit of Dallas or Port-au-Prince or Helsinki in your teeth?

Does that sliver of meat shift everything off-plumb?

Does it move you off-script? Does it move at all?

What city is this, Thames unrolling in the middle of a desert?

Mad ruin, an animal alone in its cage.

In your pasture, the networks thunder around stone & midden.

Forgotten foundations mutating into practice boundaries, a mucky ruin for cattle to rub
  their dander on.

Upriver a bag-end of drought speculators & asphalt hopefuls & years of gray topcoats &
  beyond that a flaking iron bridge that leads to a thick leather belt three inches too
  small.

Eternal not-enough, a city of skinny stares
  & beyond that a road that is a blanket beneath which thousands sleep.

Someone bakes little fables.

Moon mouth crater cut with oh meaning, depth.

Paint walls with edible blue sound dripping from the plaster when it rains.

Metal cuts dough, little hero & embroidery belt.

Strong boots, enchanted fiddle, nightingale.

Hide from the passing army in a fortuitous castle or cottage.

Nine sheep orbit the mountaintop & cloaked in fern a something watches.

That old something, snail house. Drum, oven.

Little bright lizard-stone, marking tongues pockets of opprobrium.

Licked something, silent & clean, broken out of sky & dendrite.

A vein of desire. Make it like a blood-clot, grime-encrusted window in a ghost town.

I love the way a golden light moves through a certain type of cloud.

I love the way my trash talk collects in a corner & makes a lizard.

A lizard fucks in mica sense, pierces my skin in jade crawl, makes a day into a nest, a big

    display for justice's shining scales.

She's one too.

Traffic in tease, whips, a pound of stone dust rubbed into the pores, honey, the baseball

    cards of prairie stars.

We are looking for the passage between desks & drought.

Anticipatory droplets condense about our heads.

A cup wanders from hand to hand always in need.

Tenderness is something to belong to, outstanding performer on a tightrope, a brittle cane

    on each shoulder.

When I gasp there is a reflex felt in the world's meat.

Red, throb you with the sun, down there in the hold.

Words are missing. Steal willow, steal jaguar, make plover senseless in the work of reduced scope.

Take my wolf, make him product, word product, more thing to ease trade, some owner-to-owner, business plan.

Does my disgust alarm you?

Ask yourself what that man is doing smack in the middle of your e-reader.

Ask yourself what that man could possibly be doing walking through that piece of prime undeveloped future building site.

What is his illegitimate form of existence demanding horizontal & profligate relations with space?

Words are missing, taken from the lexicon, moved into mortar for luxury residences parking garages, melted down into composite cubicles.

Words are missing. Words are missing & I too have disappeared from use, value.

This is so iffy. The little boogie-flower on the dashboard tripping, nausea.

My tears have dried, my nose is still bleeding.

On the beach waves bring plastic grocery bags to shore.

I can see this right from the highway. At speed even.

In these dog-feelings these disavowals.

Haptic blanket mess with the Orangina & nice forest of underwear in the wayback.

Driving as dick practice, pole position, prions. I love being a man.

You are about this.

You are about this limb & this barn door.

You are the work of winking, the chain-link jaw.

You are open & closed yes the way a young flower & an old flower are both open & closed.

You are moving the hand of the clock forward, back, forward.

You are the simple garden cutting through the glassed-in tower.

You.

The family of riders you carry in your chest all trumpeting your concerns, your love,

    resplendent galaxy of swords.

Sit high knees dining in emergency beside old women talk children.

We middle-aged men, together & their years.

Melted ice cap of years wash over us.

Spent forcing edges to touch when they can only part.

Forcing edges because that is what they were trained to do.

But we are salad & sandwich together & we wade in & women watch us.

My forest & your fruit

    & we rooted in their years get up, able to see one-color eye in only side, green plus

        mouth.

In a room made of hedge, blanket-strewn, one lamp. Disapproving hiss.

The battle to stay upright still fought by innovative constant renewable resources.

The hovering complex. Silent circle above the head.

Does this question make me look like a girl? Do these leaves rustle in my pants?

Like—can you hear them?

Room made of hedge not weatherproofed against hornets or insinuating strangers.

The slime of a smile dripping over the jaw, a sign begging to be taken down.

At once it's clear that the something-fabric has unraveled with one unanticipated

    divergence.

Facility of speech, map in a rough bucket dissolving noisily, we have no idea why.

One by one our skulls are illuminated from an unknown source.

Sex photos flash on the walls around us & we know ourselves in them.

Everyone wears a little badge of honor: person of interest.

Our fingers stretch toward other fingers. Just off camera we yearn impotently.

This frozen grid of our anger glaciates us into helpless preoccupation.

Those creepy nemeses shadow us with discreet devices turgid, ripple into our reflections &

    are lost.

Nourishing star, tremendous crane stretching its wings for the hope of a future forward.

A name to look through like a prism.

There are dreams that follow, soft down spiraling from the flesh of the shoulders.

A face glimpsed in a mirror with a body that moves oddly.

Bound tightly in a skin of project & define.

Say one thing & know it to be a truth. Know a truth & do not speak it.

Declare a state & hide there.

Lips made round by bright beasts of fruit.

Shape lights & drops of sound to talk in forced pattern.

All of our days made round.

Call a cul-de-sac with the lips, call it as a bus calls streets it approaches. Cul-de-sac a round street.

It's a fruit of low dark plane.

You take a rim & spin it so.

Forced pattern like grown frost.

Speak & turn. Have a growth of word, a smattering of shine on the thing being spoken.

A tongue thrust through lips made round, tongue with letters snowed along its tip.

Here, it's the room with slippery walls. Peer around the corner.

Nicety fails. Look me in the eye & tell me where you want me & I will see if that is possible.

    & if it isn't, you will be made aware of other routes.

No, that isn't what I meant to say. The misquote is serious.

I will open the door again.

Fold me, cut, shuffle. Next I open, spread on green baize with you pushing your luck into me.

Scent of risk stuck in my mustache.

Not a shark in sight & still I check the scene for blood bloom. Make me obvious.

Right: I come to the end of the known universe.

Left: the drill freezes, strips its gears, burns out the motor.

Right: hands form herds & migrate forcefully.

Left: the sea.

Right: erasure of the previous day's menu.

Left: a high-end stroller abandoned in a lift.

Right: dog food in a can, the label torn.

Left: telltale smear of paint.

Right: hippocampus.

Left: pewter jug too poisonous to use for beverages.

Right: a catalogue of deaths involving fingers.

Left: waiting.

Again the road splits into a mycelial system of intense complexity.

Nothing to do but take it all into the body, as though the indecision & bafflement nourish some vital function.

This mystery grows & the body slows with its force.

The question froths from the mouth again & again these days:

What do you want of me? From behind clenched teeth nearly every day.

How to walk a path that is both inside & outside the body & what am I right now, after all?

A door, a sparrow. Moments of English unpopular for their ambiguity.

A beveled-glass spyhole tucked just above eye-level, partially prismatic & cracking light, tumbling light about the vestibule like so many adolescent girls performing their dating dramas.

A flurry of color language, photonic & chilly.

Desperately cold silence of the door.

A zero that terrifies the outside away.

Knife-handed dust around which doubt collects, flammable drops of misery.

A way of waiting, this building. Some void encased in brick.

Read our regions in the light of coruscating tumbleweed fixtures.

This is a new something made from the smuts of burning interest, cryogenically canceled.

Analogous concerns fern out from mouths opened to investigate.

Lemon-colored apparatus on the kitchen counter, seductive, thinking & wanting.

A dry light comes through the window, enters our regions over the drawbridge of the cooker.

Does peer in, slim chins on the outer sill, making breath-candy on the other side of the glass.

Our regions pressed in & pinched, a face of dough, breached by intangibles.

Mixed plexus of days.

Drive, a machine or an inclination.

The never-noticed cracks in the concrete floor make root systems.

No central hub but what gets imposed by a brain wishing to order.

Perception, precepts, prefects of mixed-use areas.

Down on your knees. We are all gators here & make each other aware of it.

Made a hunt. A test of noise & a scene plummeting to earth. Deal & laid.

When something opens a hound thing, a bay. Take a minute to mole.

We like & like & like. A death, wrapped up.

Made a hunt in a sorcery collection.

Made a hunt in a tourist area.

Neural interface helmet & night vision.

Day folded into itself, frayed sweater crumbling into the drawer.

A saucer ringed with mice, armature of soft bodies & words.

Imperative marked with silence or wasteful knees.

Hose in hand making teams on the window.

Many days are like this, keen eye in the mirror looking sensible, looking on.

Looking out from the inside of a green-rimmed leaf hard & brittle.

The source of a wind that carries imps down from the mountains, drops them on the

    doorstep.

A shoe in the water tells the story of loss.

Abraded skin of action, sequence interrupted by gravity or the wash of white noise.

The gun that work creates, the ballistic stream of yes & maybe & absolutely no.

Dark bank overhung with discarded goods.

In a moment of future being some tool digs into the software of accumulation, projects the arms—human arms—forward many terabeats.

The heart of time makes & makes & makes again, loss that begins & ends with its lips against its own anus.

Oil, as if feathers. As if constancy of wavebreak. Length of tubing stretched & placed in grass.

Proximity. Emergent conditions, circuit.

Again, a line. Queer of dove, purslane.

Guilt works hand to paw.

O civet o bee, wax tune, drill of water against the sky.

As if feathers fall from clouds, grow vast, consume our ways.

We are all adept at breaking good silence, that frail wishbone.

We have our orange trees & our vape-houses where the presumption of entitlement

    condenses upon the walls, controls the hard bank of approval, the drift of need,

    so forth.

There is an until we wait to hear.

We hold our breath so we don't miss it.

A murmur of hope we never fail to grind into salt for unredeemed earths, & we fly from

    every opening.

Infant, excrescence, word.

Missile, ejaculate, pollen.

Soft & hard together & making more of ourselves than we can carry.

Desperate pattern of night, flashing lights through the grid of the window.

Worried about dreams & roots pushing.

The army of tyrants behind us.

Worried about animal equations & fear & longing.

Kneeling before a drowned star & its speech.

Makeshift adjustment, pastiche, approximation.

Traitor's intuition, wherein I follow my foreskin.

Card 0 shows me blithe & silly. You know the card I mean.

About to take a leap of faith, knowing just enough to put one foot before the other.

Often asked the question about planning ahead or stellar cartography.

Do you know, it's more terrifying to pretend it can be planned than it is to face a future of

    open space?

Unseeable.

In the cold there is a long bell.

The sound of a deep stress & a strong awareness.

The recurrence of a dead briar tangle in the path.

These events come regularly but with little warning.

The shocking honesty of my own eyes in the mirror.

Their blue-gray echo of the sky too low over our heads.

The whispered no as I think of what gets imposed

        & how impossible any more to pretend to be a door ringed in tinsel.

To drop my pants to the world, these hands not meant for lying.

So walk in those brief petals of light.

The palm shadows toss slivers & blades in blood-like trickles down the skin.

The wheel of becoming is at your back.

Slow spin pushing forward or maintaining equilibrium at rest, artificial gravity of a sort.

Golden hair breathes over your legs & chin, coins of meaning against the names the others

    want to apply & the days of work it takes to wash the names off, afterwards.

Thought about a hand & the teardrop expression of doom or banishment.

Flush response, shame borne on the flesh & in it, water cascading down a path.

Vision of descent.

See this emerging mist, the open mouth of panic.

Dew & palate, shattered fall of rock at feet. A created difference.

No other reason to be shunted off but to punish. & the ticking of droplets on leaves beneath

    trees & on wood.

Thought about a hand & the way it looks like the leaf of a young sassafras.

A hand outstretched & open as though inviting the palm to touch its own.

Tongue tip on the roof of the mouth, leaf pressed over the heart, a promise.

Will you approach me like a catapult so as to create a zone of meaning between us?

As mutual denizens of no exact mode or meme or bat-shaped lap of shadow on the ground,

    will you have some tea?

Is it in our dictionary, can we say love about the things we happen?

The photo in your hand, the waiting list, the mule.

Bash a nail into a tree for me maybe for us both.

What if it stings what if this contact leads to corners & evergreen poison?

What can we do our oars sprout buds we reach we reach.

What is a touch in this place what is a mouth with words in it?

You know the taste of the air when a dry hard snow strains down from a blank sky,

    shuddering & startled.

The flavor of dust beating at the back of the throat.

A little blood, a curl of hoof pared from a restless horse.

These things a language of dim heuristic questions, opalescent horizon attempting to be a

    kind of word.

The imperative of communication worthless in view of the sentience of language.

Time has the flavor of language. Nothing to be done about it.

There will always be animals & weather. What is grieved does not obscure them.

Animals & weather move around as time passes.

A buzzard circling creates a vortex. Rainfall & fish-fall.

There are sequences to be respected & monitored.

There is repetition to consider

      & in the foothills the stones murmur & grasses ten thousand years old think up

    new names for us.

We have no way to know them.

& then the clouds move away from the top of the tower.

The name erupts, a thundering cowl of hope unfurling over pedestrians & bike messengers.

The booming waves shake the streets.

A sense of breath held, waiting for a response.

The ecstatic fuel. Dreams of sexual terror.

The city opens its lungs.

The shout takes days to reach us & when it comes we hold ourselves & shudder.

Ghost of a bird, near-body flung into the air.

Shadow of motion against the sky.

The edge of a building becomes the edge of a word.

Some walk through vapor, a myth of the normal.

Deities to worship in the normal way.

What if the spirit is not a sack of grain to be filled or spent?

What if the real has no quantity?

What one desires is what one becomes, the left-behind sentence unraveling in the wake.

Pharos & map, three men in a tub.

We seek the origin of the name of the assembly.

Someone breaks bread with diviners & well-diggers, someone takes dry bones to church &
    snaps them.

Along the way a jewel is deposited in moss. A nail is exchanged for a word.

The net of documentation drags behind our party both creating & obscuring our trail.

At once there is a sudden cliff in our way.

We toss our cries over the edge, decide to turn back. Decide again.

We are whereabouts unknown possibly on the outskirts of another person's fractal utopia.

Something about this makes our backs tired.

Fried hair & peat moss, the noise of something shattering in the street below.

We are wondering battalions of underground movement in the other sense, the spelunking sense.

Find new species in that fractal utopia, similar to those secret animals discovered under the table when the special cloth reached to the floor, those days never very long gone.

Instruct me in the ways of the monster. The Santa Ana wind. The lingual work.

Beyond the sand a searing eye waits to be learned.

Find your two palms & the hum of the air surrounding the lamp.

Instruct me in the ways of parkour.

The hibiscus panting absently in the opal predawn of its late luteal phase.

No time left to knock the buildings out from under us.

This place is a mouth through which we long ago learned to speak, to promise each other

    menageries & horoscopes & light.

Dad owl takes the syllabus to task, a force to face if home is to be home.

Toads drive weekly bargains around the county for customers.

Foothills as infrastructure, foothills as resource.

Fossil stuff secret shut-in princesses, can't count on freedom in release.

Dad owl recognizes the language of thieves.

The difference between Argonaut & argotist is vehicular.

One word includes another, a load of men with weapons & doomed children, men of words

    to shatter shale.

It has called nine times. A bat tickling the pane of the bedroom window.

A long crisp snakeskin left whole upon the doorstep.

Make your meaning from these cards.

Code-breaking silences with a big dark eye.

Sudden migratory waves of sunflowers.

The information accumulates in dust. Mistakes, catalogued.

A small opening in a wall through which a hard gray tongue appears.

Vegetable wings reach from big backgrounds, contexts erupting around the origins to echo movement.

Slowly sand & wind perform like a study, maybe population changes or holidays observed.

Note two ritual cakes face to face on a shelf.

So rocks shift. Light & a smell of soil.

Hot house steaming after the straw laid down over bare roots, bone, irrigation.

Alive what motion is begun?

Alive our pleasures flow, breathed & polished like green jade.

Taken in, carried close in luminous hands. Alive.

POETICS and PROCESS: A CONVERSATION WITH JAY BESEMER

Greetings comrade! Thanks so much for talking with us about your process today. Can you introduce yourself in a way that you would choose?

I'm Jay Besemer. I'm a trans, queer poet disabled by multiple systemic chronic illnesses, currently leaving my 40s.

Why are you a poet?

I have a cheeky answer for this, which I'm going to use here: **I'm a poet because poetry is the only vehicle that allows me to simultaneously occupy all possible dimensions.**

When did you decide you were a poet (and/or: do you feel comfortable calling yourself a poet, what other titles or affiliations do you prefer/feel are more accurate)?

In many ways "poet" is the only thing I'm really totally comfortable calling myself. Everything else I am is always in addition to--or a mode of, perhaps--being a poet. I think it was always there, a way of being in the world & processing that experience, long before I claimed it as an action I committed to taking for the duration of my life.

What's a "poet", anyway?

I have a hard time answering this question consistently, & can't answer for anyone else, can't be prescriptive. So understand this as only today's, this-moment answer, from a highly unusual individual.

Simply, a poet makes poems. That is, poems result from the experiences of existence, but I don't necessarily differentiate between the existence/experience & the result/product when I use the word "poem." A poem need not be words. It's just that most people are accustomed to poems occupying a language body, accustomed to interacting with poetry that way.

What is the role of the poet today?

This is a question I can only answer for myself. I am often excluded from other people's answers because of the limits of my own physical situation & by virtue of my own poetics. I try not to be a gatekeeper for others' work needs.

What do you see as your cultural and social role (in the poetry community and beyond)?

I've been shown by others that younger trans, queer & GNC poets are finding value in my work. Increasingly poets with chronic/mental illnesses &/or who are also trauma survivors are letting me know that I'm being of service to them. This is important & unexpected, because I was under the radar for some decades, & did not have the experience of feeling I was able to be of service, or of feeling that I had any audience whatsoever.

In terms of the immediate poetry community here where I live, my role has had to change quite recently. Poetry events in general are notoriously inaccessible for disabled people, but even most mobility-accessible or Deaf/HoH accessible events are specifically inaccessible for me because of the unusual (apparently) conflux of my health, sensory, pain & fatigue conditions.

At this time, I am rarely able to participate in person, either as performer or as audience member. I observe a great interest among young poets in some of the poetry series I used to be deeply involved with, so I feel they'll continue in some way, without my involvement--I can let go, & grieve my own loss of these as means of connection. But as to what I can contribute now, I am still asking that myself. I feel like the only thing I can do--& that not even consistently--is be, & make the work, & get it out there sometimes. That has to be enough, though the poetry/activism culture tends to frame that as inadequate. This framing is deeply classist & ableist, of course, but it's still a tremendous obstacle to recognition & validation of many kinds of poetic labor. Lately I've been speaking out on that, too, primarily on Twitter.

One somewhat behind-the-scenes thing I do is to quietly make use of my contacts to connect newer writers with opportunities to publish. I do this in large part because nobody did it for me, & I worked hard in relative isolation for 25 years before my first book was published. (I was 43 at the time). I know how demoralizing that is. Again, classism! Ableism!

Talk about the process or instinct to move these poems (or your work in general) as independent entities into a body of work. How and why did this happen? Have you had this intention for a while? What encouraged and/or confounded this (or a book, in general) coming together? Was it a struggle?

I'm not sure how to answer these questions given my overall poetics/working process. But I'll talk towards the becoming of *The Ways of the Monster*.

I have been referring to this book as the third in a trilogy that began with my first book, *Telephone*, continued in my third & best-known book *Chelate*, & now wraps up with *Monster*. Originally it was formatted according to the practice I used in the other two volumes; while I was revising it for possible publication I changed that, feeling I had exhausted the purpose of the formatting & was in danger of it becoming too associated with my work--like typecasting. I didn't want something that had a deeply functional, personal purpose to become reduced to "style," or worse, to be described as "my" style. A previous version of the book had been a finalist in 2016 for the 1913 Press Open Prose period, so as I revised for that submission process I made the switch from the fragmented swarm of old into a movement in & out of declarative sentences.

This was also a response to the changes in my embodiment/movement-through-the-world at the time of its writing. Though the books in the trilogy have not been published in a direct sequence (each has been separated by a book from a different project), they were written continuously & separated into volumes at various stopping points. As my experiences of my bodymind (to use Eli Clare's great term) & its relation to the world/cosmos changed, I had to change the way that came to language in my work.

You can see it through the three volumes: *Telephone* embodies the back-&-forth swing of the time I was weighing the need to make deep changes to save my life, against my fear of doing so. (This may not be plainly spoken in the content of the book, but believe me, it's there). That was the manifestation in language of my experience in/of the world at that time. The fragmented, synesthetic, interconnecting endless sensory barrage of *Chelate* was reflected in the preservation of the textual format, without the dialectical (or feedback loop) movement of *Telephone*. But by the time *Monster* came to be--roughly two years after the writing of *Telephone*--my experiences were radically different. I was well under way in my gender transition. I was treating my chronic & mental illnesses. My body was constantly changing (& still is), but by then I'd moved out of a mode of living where I felt I must justify myself, or apologize/explain what I was, why I was myself, what made me this way. I was ready to take up space, to declare, to claim my experiences as important, as mine.

What formal structures or other constrictive practices (if any) do you use in the creation of your work? Have certain teachers or instructive environments, or readings/writings of other creative people (poets or others) informed the way you work/write?

Some of my work is sourced (cut-up, collaged or erasure work) so there are limitations to them. Generally an erasure project is limited in length by the length of its source text. I use text automation or generation programs/methods, like Markov text processors, & I have ways of misusing word processing/"productivity" apps, & other things like online forms, to generate unplanned texts. But this is not the only way I work. *Monster* was not constructed this way, nor were the other two books of the trilogy.

The most influential people in my worklife have been my poet/artist friends. Additionally I have benefited from relationships with people in other disciplines, mostly in the sciences. I also owe a lot to certain actors, whose work has deeply influenced my life & my own work, but who have not all come into my life physically.

I have made various attempts to list the most direct influences on my poetic practice over the years. Each list is different, but at the top of all of them there's always Tristan Tzara. So I'll leave him there.

Speaking of monikers, what does your title represent? How was it generated? Talk about the way you titled the book, and how your process of naming (poems, sections, etc) influences you and/or colors your work specifically.

The Ways of the Monster is titled from a line in one of its poems. This is typical of me; I'm a haphazard titler. In fact I resist titling individual poems for certain projects; this book is one of those, in keeping with the other two in the trilogy. I do seem to be a fan of section titles, though! I guess we have to have some way of navigating within a book, no matter whether we made the book or are experiencing it.

I know a lot of books have "monster" as their ethos right now. For many people, especially Black/Brown, trans &/or disabled people, the monster concept is difficult to process; it's been weaponized against us for so long, of course it's toxic! So in the book as well as its title, "monster" is used ironically & politically, much as the word "queer" is on a larger scale.
For an idea of how I'm using the word, look at its context in the poem. I also ask the unnamed interlocutor to teach me the ways of the Santa Ana wind, & of parkour. It's not possible for me to enact either of these ways, no matter how well I might be instructed! However, I have behaved monstrously, in the past; I don't need to learn how to be a monster. My monstrous past behavior reinscribed the experiences that activated my illnesses, so I'm slowly & compassionately unlearning the ways of the monster. Call it a medical application of the word. An unweaponing.

What does this particular collection of poems represent to you ...as indicative of your method/ creative practice? your history? your mission/intentions/hopes/plans?

I think I've mainly answered these already. I could add that it's a book that represents closure on one period of my life & acts as an atrium or a clearing where both reader & I can rest before proceeding into the work that comes from the current phase of my life.

What does this book DO (as much as what it says or contains)?

Some of this was explored in other answers; in some ways I can't answer the question as well as someone who doesn't know what it took to write it. I guess I need to see what it does out in the world!

What would be the best possible outcome for this book? What might it do in the world, and how will its presence as an object facilitate your creative role in your community and beyond? What are your hopes for this book, and for your practice?

I don't like to speculate or load down any project with those kinds of projections. What it does isn't up to me. It's up to readers. Especially now that I am unable to bring my body to bear in the physical spaces my books occupy, I feel there's already significant pressure for them to perform in ways I can't. Maybe that's true of all books, though.

I do hope someone gets relief, reassurance, validation, new ideas, energy from reading *The Ways of the Monster*. I hope it saves someone from feeling alone & abandoned in a punishing world. That's all I can say.

ACKNOWLEDGEMENTS & THANKS

An earlier version of *The Ways of the Monster* was a finalist in 1913 Press' 2016 Open Prose period. Thanks to the readers & editors at 1913 Press for this distinction!

Different versions of some of these pieces were previously published as follows:

"words are missing" "why would i identify" "chokehold" "pain annoyance" "blurt & burn" originally appeared in *Barzakh* Issue 7, Spring 2015. https://www.barzakh.net/spring-2015-1. Thanks to the editors for including these works in this special RAGE Issue!

"the thames" "you are about this" "lizard-stone" "will you approach me" "great holy monster" appeared in *The Journal Petra* Issue 3, Winter 2015. http://www.thejournalpetra.com/003besemer.html. Thanks to editors Olivia Cronk & Philip Sorenson for including these poems!

All my love & gratitude to Elæ [Lynne DeSilva-Johnson] for their friendship, patience, editorial chops, faith in me as poet & person, & commitment. This has been an amazing shared adventure!

Love & thanks to fellow OS kin Adrian Silbernagel, Joanna Valente & Peter Milne Greiner, for additional engagement & presence on & off page/screen.

Thanks to Johanna Hedva & John Keene, friends new & old, for spending time with me, this book, & their generous blurbs.

Thanks to those who were present/somehow involved in the process of this book's coming into being, including Laura Goldstein, Toby Altman, Kenyatta Rogers, Trace Peterson, TC Tolbert, Johannes Göransson, Joseph Bradshaw, & Daniel Borzutzsky. Thanks also to the Red Rover series & the Absinthe & Zygote series where many of these poems were "unpaged."

Thanks to Rupert Glimm, my love, whose painting graces the cover & whose life graces mine. For you, as always.

Jay Besemer's other books include *Theories of Performance* (forthcoming The Lettered Streets Press, 2019), *Crybaby City* (Spuyten Duyvil), *Telephone*, *Chelate* (both Brooklyn Arts Press), and *Aster to Daylily* (Damask Press). He was a finalist for the 2017 Publishing Triangle Award for Trans and Gender-Variant Literature. He tweets frequently @divinetailor and can be found at www.jaybesemer.net.

WHY PRINT / DOCUMENT?

*The Operating System uses the language "print document" to differentiate from the book-object as part of our mission to distinguish the act of documentation-in-book-FORM from the act of publishing as a backwards-facing replication of the book's agentive *role* as it may have appeared the last several centuries of its history. Ultimately, I approach the book as TECHNOLOGY: one of a variety of printed documents (in this case, **bound**) that humans have invented and in turn used to archive and disseminate ideas, beliefs, stories, and other evidence of production.*

Ownership and use of printing presses and access to (or restriction of printed materials) has long been a site of struggle, related in many ways to revolutionary activity and the fight for civil rights and free speech all over the world. While (in many countries) the contemporary quotidian landscape has indeed drastically shifted in its access to platforms for sharing information and in the widespread ability to "publish" digitally, even with extremely limited resources, the importance of publication on physical media has not diminished. In fact, this may be the most critical time in recent history for activist groups, artists, and others to insist upon learning, establishing, and encouraging personal and community documentation practices. Hear me out.

With The OS's print endeavors I wanted to open up a conversation about this: the ultimately radical, transgressive act of creating PRINT /DOCUMENTATION in the digital age. It's a question of the archive, and of history: who gets to tell the story, and what evidence of our life, our behaviors, our experiences are we leaving behind? We can know little to nothing about the future into which we're leaving an unprecedentedly digital document trail — but we can be assured that publications, government agencies, museums, schools, and other institutional powers that be will continue to leave BOTH a digital and print version of their production for the official record. Will we?

As a (rogue) anthropologist and long time academic, I can easily pull up many accounts about how lives, behaviors, experiences — how THE STORY of a time or place — was pieced together using the deep study of correspondence, notebooks, and other physical documents which are no longer the norm in many lives and practices. As we move our creative behaviors towards digital note taking, and even audio and video, what can we predict about future technology that is in any way assuring that our stories will be accurately told – or told at all? How will we leave these things for the record?

In these documents we say: WE WERE HERE, WE EXISTED, WE HAVE A DIFFERENT STORY

- Elæ [Lynne DeSilva-Johnson], Founder/Creative Director
THE OPERATING SYSTEM, Brooklyn NY 2018

RECENT & FORTHCOMING
OS PRINT::DOCUMENTS and PROJECTS, 2018-19

Ark Hive-Marthe Reed
I Made for You a New Machine and All it Does is Hope - Richard Lucyshyn
Illusory Borders-Heidi Reszies
A Year of Misreading the Wildcats - Orchid Tierney
We Are Never The Victims - Timothy DuWhite
Of Color: Poets' Ways of Making | An Anthology of Essays on Transformative Poetics - Amanda Galvan Huynh & Luisa A. Igloria, Editors
An Absence So Great and Spontaneous It Is Evidence of Light - Anne Gorrick
The Book of Everyday Instruction - Chloë Bass
Executive Orders Vol. II - a collaboration with the Organism for Poetic Research
One More Revolution - Andrea Mazzariello
The Suitcase Tree - Filip Marinovich
Chlorosis - Michael Flatt and Derrick Mund
Sussuros a Mi Padre - Erick Sáenz
Sharing Plastic - Blake Nemec
In Corpore Sano : Creative Practice and the Challenged Body [Anthology]
Abandoners - L. Ann Wheeler
Jazzercise is a Language - Gabriel Ojeda-Sague
Born Again - Ivy Johnson
Attendance - Rocío Carlos and Rachel McLeod Kaminer
Singing for Nothing - Wally Swist
The Ways of the Monster - Jay Besemer
Walking Away From Explosions in Slow Motion - Gregory Crosby
Field Guide to Autobiography - Melissa Eleftherion

KIN(D)* Texts and Projects

A Bony Framework for the Tangible Universe - D. Allen
Opera on TV - James Brunton
Hall of Waters - Berry Grass
Transitional Object - Adrian Silbernagel

GLOSSARIUM: Unsilenced Texts and Translations

Śnienie / Dreaming - Marta Zelwan/Krystyna Sakowicz, (Poland, trans. Victoria Miluch)
Alparegho: Pareil-À-Rien / Alparegho, Like Nothing Else - Hélène Sanguinetti
(France, trans. Ann Cefola)
High Tide Of The Eyes - Bijan Elahi (Farsi-English/dual-language)
trans. Rebecca Ruth Gould and Kayvan Tahmasebian
In the Drying Shed of Souls: Poetry from Cuba's Generation Zero
Katherine Hedeen and Víctor Rodríguez Núñez, translators/editors
Street Gloss - Brent Armendinger with translations for Alejandro Méndez, Mercedes
Roffé, Fabián Casas, Diana Bellessi, and Néstor Perlongher (Argentina)
Operation on a Malignant Body - Sergio Loo (Mexico, trans. Will Stockton)
Are There Copper Pipes in Heaven - Katrin Ottarsdóttir (Faroe Islands, trans. Matthew Landrum)
Kawsay: The Flame of the Jungle - María Vázquez Valdez (Mexico, trans. Margaret Randall)
The Book of Sounds - Mehdi Navid (Farsi dual language, trans. Tina Rahimi)
Return Trip / Viaje Al Regreso - Israel Dominguez; (Cuba, trans. Margaret Randall)

for our full catalog please visit:
https://squareup.com/store/the-operating-system/

our deeply discounted Book of the Month and Chapbook Series subscriptions
are a great way to support the OS's projects and publications!
sign up at: http://www.theoperatingsystem.org/subscribe-join/

DOC U MENT
/däkyəmənt/

First meant "instruction" or "evidence," whether written or not.

noun - a piece of written, printed, or electronic matter that provides information or evidence or that serves as an official record
verb - record (something) in written, photographic, or other form
synonyms - paper - deed - record - writing - act - instrument

[*Middle English, precept, from Old French, from Latin documentum, example, proof, from docre, to teach; see dek- in Indo-European roots.*]

Who is responsible for the manufacture of value?

Based on what supercilious ontology have we landed in a space where we vie against other creative people in vain pursuit of the fleeting credibilities of the scarcity economy, rather than freely collaborating and sharing openly with each other in ecstatic celebration of MAKING?

While we understand and acknowledge the economic pressures and fear-mongering that threatens to dominate and crush the creative impulse, we also believe that **now more than ever we have the tools to relinquish agency via cooperative means,** fueled by the fires of the Open Source Movement.

Looking out across the invisible vistas of that rhizomatic parallel country we can begin to see our community beyond constraints, in the place where intention meets resilient, proactive, collaborative organization.

Here is a document born of that belief, sown purely of imagination and will.
When we document we assert. We print to make real, to reify our being there.
When we do so with mindful intention to address our process, to open our work to others, to create beauty in words in space, to respect and acknowledge the strength of the page we now hold physical, a thing in our hand, we remind ourselves that, like Dorothy: *we had the power all along, my dears.*

THE PRINT! DOCUMENT SERIES

is a project of
the trouble with bartleby
in collaboration with
the operating system

www.ingramcontent.com/pod-product-compliance
Lightning Source LLC
Chambersburg PA
CBHW080025130526
44591CB00037B/2674